Dedication

To "My Girls",

I see you once a year for your well exams - maybe more if you come in the office sick. And we discuss issues of heart and body. Many of you struggle with the way you look in some way or another, and I think all of you want to be accepted as beautiful.

I want so desperately for each of you to know that our Heavenly Father took such great care when He made you and chose how you would look. That you are already beautiful. I want you to know and experience how wide, how long, how high, and how deep He loves you; that you are never out of his reach. I want you to know that He has a purpose and plan for your life. That you are so precious to Him. YOU ARE CHERISHED.

Contents

Introduction

I am so humbled that you picked up this study. I have worked with teenage girls for many years as a healthcare provider and a confidant in their personal and spiritual lives. Through my practice and personal experience growing up, I know the struggle to feel beautiful, the desire to be loved and accepted, as well as the temptation to do anything to feel like you are.

Inspired by my most common conversations with teen girls, this journey began as a guided Bible Study and flourished into this book for self-study. I pray that as you make your way through this that you can see how skewed our culture has become and learn to realign your view with God's perspective of who you are and who He made you to be - cherished beyond comprehension!

Chapter 1

Formed by God

I once knew a girl who had to wear what was in style and fix her hair just right. She compared herself with others and thought she needed to be a certain weight and size clothing. She disliked her "wide Aunt Lucy hips" and her nose that was too big. She was self-conscious of her ears that the boys deemed "satellite ears" as they pretended to tune in to ESPN. Once her growth-spurt hit, she was a head taller than everyone else and had changes in her body that she attempted to cover up with large T-shirts and slouching. She had such a longing to be beautiful and accepted and everything on her body to be in proportion — just like the models.

Have you ever struggled with your appearance? I know I have — many times. And to be honest, I overcome it and then it comes back in a different form at a different stage of life. So while I wrote this with younger teenage girls in mind, I also am revisiting some issues in my own life and letting the Truth seep into my soul. God's Word promises that the Truth will set you free. I pray this does the same for you.

First, we are going to look at the great care God took in molding our bodies, deciding how He wanted us to look. Think of a sculptor. He or she spends weeks or months molding this ball of clay, examining every square inch, taking off a little here, adding a little there until it looks juuuuusst right.

In the same way, our Heavenly Father formed you. He picked out your eyes, nose, ears, lips, hair color, skin tone … He did not carelessly throw you together.

Here's some Scripture so you can see this for yourself. Psalm 139:13-18 (NASB, emphasis mine):

> 13 For You **formed** my inward parts;
>
> You wove me in my mother's womb.
>
> 14 I will give thanks to You, for I am **fearfully** and **wonderfully** made;
>
> Wonderful are Your **works**,
>
> And my soul knows it **very well**.
>
> 15 My frame was not hidden from You,
>
> When I was made in **secret**,
>
> And **skillfully wrought** in the depths of the earth;
>
> 16 Your eyes have seen my unformed substance;
>
> And in Your book were **all written**
>
> The days that were **ordained** for me,
>
> When as yet there was not one of them.
>
> 17 How **precious** also are Your **thoughts** to me, O God!
>
> How vast is the sum of them!
>
> 18 If I should count them, they would outnumber the sand.
>
> When I awake, I am still with you.

Now, you may have noticed some words stand out more than others. On the next page is a chart with the meaning of those words in the original language. You may be wondering why you would need to know this.

The Bible was originally written in a different language and sometimes the true meaning of the words cannot be fully described when translated into English. (Side note — I like charts. Sometimes they are easier on the eyes than a bunch of words. And although I love to read, I also like visual aids and charts help me remember. So, a chart for you! Are you as excited as I am?). Read through these definitions:

WORD	MEANING
formed	originating from God[1] (man had nothing to do with it)
fearfully	to cause astonishment and awe; to inspire Godly reverence, respect, and honor[2]
wonderfully	distinguished; set apart[3]
works	what has been accomplished[4] (God's formation of you)
very well	exceedingly abundant[5] (to me this is overflowing reassurance; no doubt)
secret	literally secret, but also shelter or protection[6] (God made the environment of the mother's womb to be a place of protection for unborn babies)
skillfully wrought	mix colors; variegate[7] (each color of your body was mixed by God specifically for you!)
all	whole, total, anything and everything[8]
written	recorded, inscribed, engraved[9] (it cannot be erased)
ordained	for divine (Godly) purpose[10]
precious	to be highly valued or prized[11]
thoughts	thoughts and purposes[12]

Again you may be thinking, "Ok?". But let's re-read the Scripture with these meanings inserted:

[13] For God formed your inward parts. They originated from Him.
God wove you together in your mother's womb.

[14] Give thanks to Him, for you are made in a way that is to inspire
Godly respect and honor. You are distinguished, set apart.
Wonderful are God's works of creating you. Your soul knows it

exceedingly, abundantly well with overflowing reassurance.

¹⁵ Your frame or bones were not hidden from God when you were fashioned in the secret protection of your mother's womb and when your colors were mixed in the depths of the earth.

¹⁶ God's eyes have seen your unformed substance and in His book are engraved anything and everything about the days of your life with a Godly purpose. This recording happened before any of your days had yet come.

¹⁷ How highly valued or prized are God's thoughts and purposes for you. How numerous is the sum of them.

¹⁸ If you should count them, they would outnumber the sand. When you awake, He is still with you.

Well, I don't know about you, but to me that has a whole new meaning! Can you see how much thought God put into you and your purpose — even before you were born? I sure hope so!

Let's take it further. This passage in Psalm teaches us some things about God that I want you to understand personally:

- God formed you (v. 13).
- God sees you (v. 16).
- God has a purpose for you (vv. 16-17).
- God values you as his prized possession (vv. 17-18).

GOD FORMED YOU

Didn't I say at the beginning that God did not carelessly throw you together? Job 10:10-12 tells us "You guided my conception and formed me in the womb. You clothed me with skin and flesh, and you knit my bones and sinews together. You gave me life and showed me your unfailing love. My life was preserved by your care."

Here are a few passages that talk about how God formed you. There are two things I want you to take note of in Genesis 1:

1. God spoke everything — except people —- into being. Genesis 1 (ESV) repeatedly tells us "And God said ... and it was so." This is how God proceeded to create all things — day and night; heavens and ocean; land and seas and plants; sun, moon, and stars; fish and birds; and land animals.

2. There is a larger amount of text dedicated to the formation of humans compared to the rest of Creation. God's formation of humans was the epitome of His Creation, meaning His value of us and purpose for us is greater than say, the trees or birds.

The following chapter of Genesis goes into a little more detail about the creation of man. Genesis 2:7 (ESV) says, "Then the LORD God formed the man from the dust of the ground and breathed into his nostrils the breath of life, and the man became a living creature." God spoke all of creation into being, but when He created the first people, He actually formed them from dust and breathed life into them! Job 33:4 (ESV) says, "For the Spirit of God has made me, and the breath of the Almighty gives me life."

From these two passages, we learn that God gave us life with His breath. Another way He made us is in His image.

> Genesis 1:27: "So God created human beings in his own image. In the image of God he created them; male and female he created them."

> Genesis 5:1b: "When God created human beings, he made them to be like himself."

What do you think it means to be made in God's image?

Genesis 1:26-28 tells us that God gave humans authority over all creation. This means we are to responsibly care for the things He created. A few chapters later, Genesis 3:22 tells us we have the capacity to know right from wrong. No other created thing has this intellectual ability. And just to give you one more piece about this — many Bible scholars believe that being made in God's image also has to do with His character traits that He bestows on us: love, joy, patience, kindness toward others; also personality and creativity; the ability to reason. But the first two things mentioned (responsibility over all other creation, and ability to know right from wrong), the Bible actually spells out about being made in the image of God.

GOD SEES YOU

The next thing our main text teaches is that God sees you. Verse 16 says, "Your eyes have seen my unformed substance…" Earlier in this same chapter of Psalm it speaks of God's all-seeing power and how we cannot escape from Him.

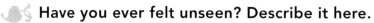 **Have you ever felt unseen? Describe it here.**

Read Psalm 139:1-4 in your Bible.

Wherever you are today, whatever you are struggling with, when you just want someone to know you exist — know that your Heavenly Father sees you.

GOD HAS A PURPOSE FOR YOU

The third thing from Psalm 139 we see about God is that He has a purpose for you. Deuteronomy 32:4 says, "He is the Rock; his deeds are perfect. Everything he does is just and fair. He is a faithful God who does no wrong; how just and upright He is!"

Did you hear that? He does no wrong. He does not make mistakes. He did not make a mistake when he created you. Do not let anyone tell you that you were an accident. Your life was carefully planned out by the Creator God.

Now I do want to quickly address something here. You may have a rough life and have been through more than I can imagine. I just want to say that bad things do happen; but bad things do not come from God. Just know that God can use bad things to bring blessing. My pastor once said it this way, "Sometimes God allows us to go down pathways we would never choose, to experience blessings we could never imagine."[13]

Describe a time when you've seen God take a bad experience or situation and turn it into good.

GOD VALUES YOU AS HIS PRIZED POSSESSION

The last thing we learn about God is that He values you. In Isaiah 43:1,4 God is speaking to His chosen people — the Israelites, also known as Jacob. It says, "But now, O Jacob, listen to the LORD who created you. O Israel, the one who formed you says, 'Do not be afraid for I have ransomed you. I have called you by name; you are mine … Others were given in exchange for you. I traded their lives for yours because you are precious to me. You are honored, and I love you."

Can you hear the passion in His voice? That is the same love and passion the Lord has for you! Again in Isaiah, God is speaking to His chosen people:

Isaiah 46:3-4b, "I have cared for you since you were born. Yes, I carried you before you were born. I will be your God throughout your lifetime — until your hair is white with age. I made you, and I will care for you. I will carry you along and save you."

Isaiah 49:1, "The LORD called me before my birth; from within the womb he called me by name."

Psalm 71:6, "Yes, you have been with me from birth; from my mother's womb you have cared for me. No wonder I am always praising you."

Can you see it? Oh dear one, I hope you can! God cares so deeply for you!

So we just have walked through how God formed you, how He sees you, how He has a purpose for you, and how He values you as His prized possession. Those things should elicit a personal response. According to Psalm 139, you should:

- have a relationship with Him (v. 18).
- thank Him, be in awe of/honor/respect Him (v. 14).
- be set apart for Him (v. 14).
- acknowledge Him (vv. 13-14).
- live out His purpose for your life (v. 16).

HAVE A RELATIONSHIP WITH HIM

You may be wondering what it means to have a relationship with God. To have a relationship with God is first to accept that you are sinful, believe that Christ paid the necessary price for your sins, and commit your life to God. This is more than just going to church or doing good things. This is praying and reading the Bible regularly, seeking God's way for your life, and following His will above all else. Having a relationship with God is truly the foundation to living a fulfilling life. When you have a relationship with God, He will remind you how much He values you.

THANK HIM, BE IN AWE OF/HONOR/RESPECT HIM

You have seen how God took great care in knitting you together and how God thought enough of you to make you in His image and use His breath to give you life. In response to that, you should appreciate His work of art.

Genesis 1:22 says that God blessed the man and woman, and verse 31 says that God looked over everything He had made and it was all very good. And "since everything God created is good, we should not reject any of it but receive it with thanks" (1 Timothy 4:4).

Along those lines, don't compare yourself to someone else. We just read that He formed you individually and to fulfill a special purpose He has for you specifically. When you compare your life or your body to others it does not honor or respect God, and only makes you ungrateful to Him and down on yourself. Romans 9:20, "Who are you, a mere human being to argue with God? Should the thing that was created say to the one who created it, 'Why have you made me like this?' "

What is a part of your body that you struggle to like? Remember you were specially formed by God. You are fearfully and wonderfully made. Tell yourself this until you start believing it.

BE SET APART FOR HIM

We will go into more detail in the coming chapters on what exactly this means. But for now, the basic idea behind this is that God's people are to think and act differently from the rest of the world. He wants us to be set apart as Holy.

ACKNOWLEDGE HIM

The simple fact that the word "formed" in this case means originating from

God; you can't deny God's involvement in the creation of you and in your life. This act of acknowledging Him, leads to worship.

LIVE OUT HIS PURPOSE FOR YOUR LIFE

Without knowing God, you cannot know His purpose for you. This is another area we will discuss more in Chapter 3.

Do you remember the girl I mentioned at the beginning of the chapter? That was me, looking to peers to validate me. As my relationship with the Lord flourished and He worked in my heart, I acknowledged Him as my Creator and learned to accept my "wide Aunt Lucy hips" seeing that God gave them to me for childbirth ... even though that was faaaarrrrr off (farther off than I expected, too. Another story for another time). I thought I had turned to God for my confidence and then soon after I got married, I looked to my husband to affirm me. After all, if anyone should think I was valuable or beautiful, it should be my husband, right? And the status of being "married" was now part of my identity.

Well, shortly after marriage, I found out that he was into pornography (which he no longer struggles with, thanks to the Lord's help). How was I to compare with pictures that had been airbrushed and perfected through technology? They didn't have *cellulite*! It was during this time that I really began to lean into God and find my worth in who I am in His eyes. I realized that people will let you down; God will not. I had idolized my husband and put him on a pedestal and he let me down. But because I had a relationship with God, He validated me.

So I state it again: don't look to others to approve of you or find your confidence in who they say you are. Look to God, the one who formed you, the one who always loves you, the one who values you.

Discussion Questions:

1. Have you ever struggled with your appearance or purpose in life? Have you ever felt unseen?

2. Has anyone ever made you feel worthless or told you that you were a mistake? How did you feel and has your perspective of that changed since reading this chapter?

3. What does it mean to be made in the image of God?

4. Describe a time when you've seen God use a bad experience or situation and turn it into good.

5. What does it mean to have a relationship with God?

6. What are some practical ways of being set apart for God?

7. Who are you looking to validate you?

Chapter 2

True Beauty

Beauty. What or who do you think of when you hear that word? Do you feel beautiful? If not, what would it take for you to feel beautiful? You may be thinking things like long, thick eyelashes or a pretty dress, or makeup — lots of makeup. Or you may be thinking about a particular illness or condition you have that has altered your appearance and prevents you from feeling beautiful. Or maybe you wish you were taller or shorter, thinner or more plump. I already told you I have struggled with these things — and sometimes still do. But to help you figure out the meaning of true beauty, I want to start by reading about one of the most famous women in the Bible. And guess what? She doesn't even have a name.

Read Proverbs 31:10-31.

What stands out to you about this woman?

Do you think she is beautiful? If so, why?

What does it mean to "laugh without fear of the future"?

Just in case you're wondering the answer to that question — the Proverbs 31 woman can laugh without fear of the future because she trusts in God's provision.

From this passage, we can categorize this woman's life into four areas and find the attributes she exhibits in each one. Let's look at these together.

How she interacts with her husband:

- Precious (verse 10)

- Trustworthy (verse 11)

- Greatly enriches his life (verse 11)

- Brings him good, not harm (verse 12)

How she values work:

- Resourceful (verses 13-14, 16)

- Productive (verses 13, 18-19) — she is "busy" but she is busy in a way that is beneficial, not just wasting time

- Organized (verse 15) — gets up early to plan and prepare

- Hard worker (verse 17)

- Profitable (verse 18)

- Likely wealthy (verse 22) — in Biblical times, purple was a very expensive dye and reserved for royalty, priests, and officials[14]

How she interacts with others:

- Generous (verse 20)

- Cares for those in her home (verse 21)

- Well-known in the community (verses 23-24)

- Speaks with wisdom and kindness (verse 26)

- Aware of all happenings in the home (verse 27)

How she carries herself:

- Energetic (verse 17)

- Strong (verses 17, 25)

- Dignified (verse 25)

- Trusts God with her future (verse 25)
- Not lazy (verse 27)

Wow! And if that isn't enough, she is blessed by her children, praised by her husband, and known and rewarded publicly by her achievements and dealings (verses 28-29, 31). She is accepted and loved by her family and community who sing her praises. Isn't this one of our deepest desires — to be accepted and loved? I know it is for me. "In our society where physical appearance counts for so much, it may surprise us to realize that her appearance is never mentioned. Her attractiveness comes entirely from her character."[15] Let that sink in: Her attractiveness comes entirely from her character! I don't know about you, but I want to be like her. And I think she is probably the most gorgeous woman you'll ever meet. Let's move on to some other Scriptures that further define beauty.

WHAT BEAUTY IS NOT

Proverbs 11:22: "A beautiful woman who lacks discretion is like a gold ring in a pig's snout."

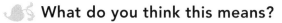 **What do you think this means?**

It took me a while to grasp the meaning of this. Would you agree that gold is valuable? Well what good is it in a pig's nose? Not very much. The same goes for beauty. If you see a "beautiful" woman but she cannot make good decisions, her beauty becomes worthless. This tells us that true beauty is *not* lack of discretion, and you should be careful of the choices you make.

In Esther 1:11-12 (ESV), the King of Persia was holding a great feast and sent for his queen: "to bring Queen Vashti before the king with her royal crown, in order to show the peoples and the princes her beauty, for she was lovely to look at. But Queen Vashti refused to come at the king's command delivered by the eunuchs. At this the king became enraged, and his anger burned within him."

In this situation, a queen — who was beautiful from the world's perspective — disobeyed the king, which ultimately publicly disrespected him and showed her lack of loyalty toward him. This shows that true beauty is *not* disrespect, disobedience, or disloyalty, and that you should do the opposite: show respect, loyalty and honor to others — especially to your husband when you get to that stage of life.

In Matthew 23:25-28, Jesus is speaking to the religious people who kept trying to trap Him in His teachings. They were so focused on keeping the religious laws they could not see the heart behind the laws. He says to them:

> What sorrow awaits you teachers of religious law and you Pharisees. Hypocrites! For you are so careful to clean the outside of the cup and the dish, but inside you are filthy – full of greed and self-indulgence! You blind Pharisee! First wash the inside of the cup and the dish, and then the outside will become clean too. What sorrow awaits you teachers of religious law and you Pharisees. Hypocrites! For you are like whitewashed tombs – beautiful on the outside but filled on the inside with dead people's bones and all sorts of impurity. Outwardly you look like righteous people, but inwardly your hearts are filled with hypocrisy and lawlessness.

Wow! What a rebuke! This is talking about outward appearance versus what's in the heart. Yes you can put on a face and make people think you are something you truly aren't. Jesus says what matters is what's in the heart. So from this you see that beauty is *not* outward appearance, and that you should fill your heart — or inside — with good things, then the outside will be good too.

So I have just presented you with three passages of Scripture that show us what beauty is not and the application for us. And to make it a quick reference, fill in the following chart with what you've just learned.

Scripture Passage	Beauty Is NOT	Application for Me
Proverbs 11:22		
Esther 1:11-12		
Matthew 23:25-28		

WHAT BEAUTY IS

So now I want us to look at some Scriptures that tell us what beauty *is* to God.

In 1 Samuel 16, the prophet Samuel is about to anoint the next king of Israel. The Lord told him to go to a man named Jesse, for one of his sons would be the king. Then one by one all of Jesse's sons paraded in front of Samuel to see if he was to be the anointed king of Israel. Verse 7 says, "But the LORD said to Samuel, 'Don't judge by his appearance or height, for I have rejected him. The LORD doesn't see things the way you see them. People judge by outward appearance, but the LORD looks at the heart.' " The Lord chose the least likely — from a human's perspective — of Jesse's sons to be the king. To people, he didn't have the appearance of a king. This is similar to what we were just reading, that beauty is not outward appearance. This passage shows that beauty *is* character and matters of the heart, and you should fill your heart with good things. At the same time you should not judge other people by how they look.

1 Timothy 2:9-10: "And I want women to be modest in their appearance. They should wear decent and appropriate clothing and not draw attention to themselves by the way they fix their hair or by wearing gold or pearls or expensive clothes. For women who claim to be devoted to God should make themselves attractive by the good things they do."

Now, is it ok to fix your hair, dress nicely or wear jewelry? (Just a side note — my grandparents and dad were jewelers. I like sparkly things, ok?) The point here is you should dress for yourself, not so someone else will notice you; and dress modestly, not to draw attention to your curves. That is not the kind of attention you deserve from boys or anyone else. From this Scripture we learn that beauty is modesty and the good things you do.

1 Peter 3:3-5 says, "Don't be concerned about the outward beauty of fancy hairstyles, expensive jewelry, or beautiful clothes. You should clothe yourselves instead with the beauty that comes from within, the unfading beauty of a gentle and quiet spirit, which is so precious to God. This is how the holy women of old made themselves beautiful. They trusted God and accepted the authority of their husbands."

Doesn't this sound like the woman in Proverbs 31 we read about at the beginning?

 What does it mean to have a gentle and quiet spirit?

A gentle and quiet spirit refers to your disposition toward others and toward God. You should not always try to get your way, and you should accept God's ways — even if it hurts — knowing that He can use it for good and to bring glory to His Name. This Scripture specifically states that beauty *is* a gentle and quiet spirit, that you should trust God and accept the authority of your husband (when you get to that stage).

So just like you did with the what beauty is *not* section, sum up what beauty *is* and how you can apply it to your life. Fill in the following chart with what you've just learned.

Scripture Passage	Beauty IS	Application for Me
1 Samuel 16:7		
1 Timothy 2:9-10		
1 Peter 3:3-5		

I hope that gave you a new perspective on true beauty and how we can make the most of our beauty. I mentioned in the last chapter not to compare yourself with others and this is why: the world doesn't know the meaning of true beauty, and the world's opinions are constantly changing. Think of fashion — this year it was skinny jeans, next year it will be bell-bottoms; one year it's thin eyebrows, the next big bushy eyebrows or a unibrow — ok maybe not a unibrow, but do you see my point? The world changes. But listen to this: God never changes. His opinion of who we are and who we should be never changes. And I have just shown you what He thinks is beautiful.

I would encourage you at this point to do a self-evaluation. Are you beautiful on the inside — or are you more concerned with your outward appearance?

Discussion Questions

1. Who or what do you think of when you hear the word "beauty"?

2. Do you feel beautiful? If not, what would it take for you to feel beautiful?

3. What stands out to you about the Proverbs 31 woman? Do you think she is beautiful? If so, why?

4. What does it mean to "laugh without fear of the future"?

5. Explain Proverbs 11:22.

6. What does it mean to have a gentle and quiet spirit?

7. Self-evaluation. Are you beautiful on the inside or are you more concerned with your outward appearance?

Chapter 3

God's Purpose for You

In the first chapter, I showed you how you were made *by* God. In this chapter, I am going to discuss His purpose and plan for you and how you were made *for* God. I'm not sure about you but I personally am a planner and the future tends to be something I want to know. How is this situation going to work out? What will I be doing in five years? Ten years? This is *my* plan for how so-and-so is going to happen. But I have seen over and over how *God's* purpose prevails over my plans. Proverbs 19:21 (ESV) "Many are the plans in the mind of a man, but it is the purpose of the Lord that will stand."

In the Old Testament, God's people had been taken captive in Babylon for 70 years. While they were there, this is what the Lord spoke through the prophet Jeremiah (29:11-13): " 'For I know the plans I have for you,' says the LORD. 'They are plans for good and not disaster, to give you a future and a hope. In those days when you pray, I will listen. If you look for me wholeheartedly, you will find me.' "

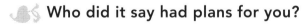 **Who did it say had plans for you?**

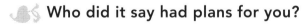 **What 3 things did God say his plans are for?**

The first part said that God knows the plans He has for you. NOT God knows the plans you have for you, although He does. What about your mom? Does she have a plan for you? She wants you to be doctor or lawyer, play soccer or piano? It did not say that God knows the plans your mom has for you, although He knows that too. Nor did it say you know the plans God has for you. But you can, and I'll tell you more about how to do that later.

The verse said God knows the plans He has for you. And they are plans for good, a future, and a hope. I hope if you are a type-A person like me that you can sigh in relief. Whatever you are trying to control or are stressing over, God's got this!

Before I tell you how to know God's specific purpose for you, you must know God's all-encompassing purpose for you. Have you ever thought about your future? Have you thought of getting married someday? I remember being young and dreaming about my wedding; what the setting would be, what style dress I would wear … Well, the Bible tells us that those who believe in Jesus Christ are His bride. Isaiah 62:3-4 is talking of God's people as a whole: "The Lord will hold you in his hand for all to see — a splendid crown in the hand of God … Your new name will be 'The City of God's Delight' and 'The Bride of God,' for the Lord delights in you and will claim you as his bride."

Psalm 45:11 says, "For your royal husband delights in your beauty; honor him, for he is your lord."

Both of these talk about how God delights in His people. He delights in your beauty.

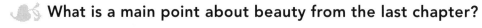 **What is a main point about beauty from the last chapter?**

When you become a Christ follower, He gives you a pure white gown to wear. He places a crown on your head and calls you His own.

You see, until you believe in Christ, you are blemished. You are broken. You are unsatisfied, defiled by your sin, shame, and the wrong things you have done. This is your inner nature — the way you were born. You may be wondering if God created you to be sinful. The answer is no! But the first two people he created *chose* to disobey Him and at that moment, they became blemished and were separated from a Holy God. And through them, the rest of the human race is born sinful rather than holy. But the story doesn't end there.

God is compassionate and wants everyone to be in fellowship with Him. So He provided a way for that to happen: He sent His Son Jesus to live on earth as a human. Jesus faced the same struggles that you do today, but He overcame them without sinning — without messing up. People became angry with Him and murdered Him, and three days later — because He had God's power — He rose from the dead. Because He lived as a perfect human, and at the same time was deity, through His supernatural death and resurrection, He bridged the gap for you to be at peace with God. When you believe in Jesus, it means that you trust that He took upon himself your penalty for the wrong things you have done and you are free of that consequence. He takes your stained, blemished, messy, sinful, shameful life and replaces it with perfect beauty and makes you His bride. I'm not going to go down a rabbit trail here, but — you will still mess up and make mistakes. However, your heart, mind, and soul have been transformed to the point that when you die and stand before a Holy and Righteous God, you are seen by God as Holy, blameless, spotless — the Bride of Christ.

As the Bride of Christ, you have an inheritance promised to you by God (Hebrews 9:15). Psalm 37:18 tells us that this inheritance lasts forever — it is eternal. First Peter 1:4 gives more detail. It says, "and we have a priceless inheritance — an inheritance that is kept in heaven for you, pure and undefiled, beyond the reach of change and decay." Your body will eventually change and decay. You will get wrinkles and gray hair, but if you are in Christ, you have an inheritance that cannot be touched by the effects of this sinful world! It is secure in heaven. Pure. Unchanging. Unfading. It never loses it's sparkle! If you believe in Christ, this inheritance is waiting on you in heaven.

So as the Bride of Christ, you have an inheritance. You also have a responsibility here and now. You must know Him. Just because you have knowledge *about* God or go to church does not mean you automatically get to be the Bride or have the inheritance.

Let me give you an example. There's a girl at school named Lauren. You know that Lauren has blonde hair and blue eyes and is of average height. She tends to do well in class and plays on the basketball team. You have knowledge *about* Lauren. But there's another girl named Kate. Kate is tall with brown eyes and brown curly hair. She also does well in school. Kate is your best friend. You have stayed at her house. The two of you have shared secrets. You know her favorite color, the makeup of her family, what makes her happy and what frustrates her. You have a *relationship* with Kate.

This is what God desires of you — to *know Him*, not just know *about* Him. And you must make a decision for yourself to give your life to what God wants you to do. Remember Jeremiah 29:11-13 from the beginning of this chapter? God has a plan. You just don't always know all of it. How do you get to know His plan for you? Verses 12-13 of that chapter say to pray and seek Him wholeheartedly and you will find Him. Proverbs 3:5-6 tells you to "trust in the LORD with all your heart, do not lean on your own understanding. In all your ways acknowledge him, and he will make your paths straight." You must acknowledge or know Him, and *then* He will make his way known to you.

Jeremiah 32:39 speaks a little about God's purpose for His people, "And I will give them one heart and one purpose: to worship me forever, for their own good and for the good of all their descendants."

I mentioned earlier how He transforms your heart when you decide to follow

Him:

> Ezekiel 11:19-20: "And I will give them singleness of heart and give them a tender, responsive heart, so they will obey My decrees and regulations. Then they will truly be My people, and I will be their God."

> Jeremiah 24:7: "I will give them hearts that recognize me as the LORD. They will be my people, and I will be their God, for they will return to me wholeheartedly."

You literally have a heart transplant when you come to know God and surrender your life to Him. God desires a relationship with you. Now let's refer back to Jeremiah 29:11-13.

 **What happens when we pray?**

What happens when we eagerly seek God?

When we pray, God listens. When we seek Him, He promises we will find Him. As you seek to know God, He will let you know His secrets, His plans for you. The responsibility is on Him to reveal it in His time. Your responsibility is to seek Him. You can make plans for your life, but more importantly seek God's purpose and be willing to go wherever He leads — which sometimes may not be your plan.

Remember from the beginning that His plans are for good, not harm. I also want you to know that He can use bad situations for good. In Jeremiah, God's people were not in a good situation — they were prisoners of war. But God reassured them that He was still in control, He had a plan for their future and a hope for them, and that He heard their prayers.

Romans 8:28: "And we know that God causes everything to work together for the good of those who love God and are called according to his purpose for them."

Isaiah 55:8-9: " 'My thoughts are nothing like your thoughts,' says the LORD. 'And my ways are far beyond anything you could imagine. For just as the heavens are higher than the earth, so my ways are higher than your ways and my thoughts higher than your thoughts.' "

Remember, you are broken and blemished and defiled and He can turn you into a beautiful, spotless, blameless bride. You must first believe in Jesus and trust that God has a better plan for your life than you do — even when it doesn't make sense — and then you seek Him and allow Him to use your mess for good.

Discussion Questions

1. Who has plans for your life?

2. What 3 things did God say His plans are for?

3. What is a main point of beauty from the last chapter?

4. What does it mean to be the Bride of Christ?

5. What happens when we pray?

6. What happens when we eagerly seek God?

7. What is God's main purpose for your life?

8. What is one thing you want to remember about God's plan?

Chapter 4

Purity

In chapter 1, I mentioned that God's people are to be set apart for Him and they are to be holy, and in chapter 3, I talked about being made for God. In this chapter, I am going to delve deeper into what exactly that means. We will be dissecting Romans 12:1-2 and using other scriptures to explain them, but always coming back to these two verses. It may be a little intense. Are you ready? Here's the main text:

Romans 12:1-2:

> [1] And so, dear brothers and sisters, I plead with you to give your bodies to God because of all he has done for you. Let them be a living and holy sacrifice — the kind he will find acceptable. This is truly the way to worship him.
>
> [2] Don't copy the behavior and customs of this world, but let God transform you into a new person by changing the way you think. Then you will learn to know God's will for you, which is good and pleasing and perfect.

"AND SO"

This passage begins with a transition phrase "and so." Other translations may use the word "therefore." Both of these mean the thought is continuing from something previously mentioned. Anytime you see the word "therefore" you must back up to see what it is "there for." Got it? Ok. So back up to Romans 11:36. Well, it begins with "for," so let's back up a little further to verse 33.

🔖 **Read Romans 11:33 in your Bible.**

And now verse 36 says, "For everything comes from him and exists by his power and is intended for his glory. All glory to him forever! Amen." We have already talked about that! From Him. By Him. For Him.

"AND SO … I PLEAD WITH YOU TO GIVE YOUR BODIES TO GOD"

🔖 **Why does the author use the word "bodies" in verse 1?**

He could have said heart or mind. Your body encompasses all of you; the whole. God doesn't want just an arm or just an eye.

🔖 **Read 1 Corinthians 6:19-20 in your Bible.**

🔖 **What must you do with your body?**

Romans 6:13 says, "Do not let any part of your body become an instrument of evil to serve sin. Instead, give yourselves completely to God, for you were dead, but now you have new life. So use your whole body as an instrument to do what is right for the glory of God."

🔖 **What did that verse say you must do with your body?**

"BECAUSE OF ALL HE HAS DONE FOR YOU"

Back to Romans 12:1. It says "I plead with you to give your bodies to God." Why? "because of all he has done for you."

 What has God/Christ done for you?

Romans 3:25 says, "For God presented Jesus as the sacrifice for sin. People are made right with God when they believe that Jesus sacrificed his life, shedding his blood."

Let's go a little deeper. Picture a baptism as you read this from Romans 6:4,6: "For we died and were buried with Christ by baptism. And just as Christ was raised from the dead by the glorious power of the Father, now we also may live new lives ... We know that our old sinful selves were crucified with Christ so that sin might lose its power in our lives. We are no longer slaves to sin."

Your baptism symbolizes your death, burial, and resurrection through Christ. When you accept Him you are given new life and new power to defeat sin. Sin has no power in your life if you are a believer!

"LET THEM BE A LIVING AND HOLY SACRIFICE — THE KIND HE WILL FIND ACCEPTABLE"

First, let's answer the question "What is a sacrifice?" A sacrifice is giving up something in order to gain something else. What you give up must have value — it's going to cost you something; otherwise it would be a donation or gift, rather than a sacrifice.

1 Peter 1:14-16: "So you must live as God's obedient children. Don't slip back into your old sinful ways of living to satisfy your own desires.

You didn't know any better then. But now you must be holy in everything you do, just as God who chose you is holy. For the Scriptures say, 'You must be holy because I am holy.' "

Giving up your desires to follow God's desires *is* a sacrifice and "truly the way to worship him" according to our text.

Romans 8:13 (ESV): "If you live according to the flesh (sinful nature) you will die, but if by the Spirit (new life in Christ's power) you put to death the deeds of the body, you will live."

As a believer with the help of the indwelling Holy Spirit, you let go of your fleshly desires and worldly pleasures by not giving in to temptations. The result is that God is pleased and the Bible tells us there is also a reward for that in heaven.

"DON'T COPY THE BEHAVIORS AND CUSTOMS OF THIS WORLD"

This is more of what we were just discussing. And we could go into a lot of detail here, but generally speaking, it refers to anything that doesn't please God. More specifically, I'll just let you fill in the blank and let's move on because we will come back to this at the end.

"BUT LET GOD TRANSFORM YOU INTO A NEW PERSON BY CHANGING THE WAY YOU THINK"

Ephesians 4:23-24: "Instead, let the Spirit renew your thoughts and attitudes. Put on your new nature, created to be like God — truly righteous and holy."

Colossians 3:10: "Put on your new nature, and be renewed as you learn to know your Creator and become like him."

 What do these Scriptures say must happen in order for you to be renewed?

Both of these passages suggest that in order to be renewed in the Spirit, you must put on your new nature in Christ.

◇

Romans 8:5-6 says, "Those who are dominated by the sinful nature think about sinful things, but those who are controlled by the Holy Spirit think about things that please the Spirit. So letting your sinful nature control your mind leads to death. But letting the Spirit control your mind leads to life and peace."

"THEN YOU WILL LEARN TO KNOW GOD'S WILL FOR YOU, WHICH IS GOOD AND PLEASING AND PERFECT"

When? Then. After all this other stuff we have discussed has taken place. In short, once you become a believer, you are given the Holy Spirit, Who gives you power to overcome sin and also shows you right from wrong. Through the process of obeying the Spirit's prompting in your life (not giving in to temptations), the Spirit will change the way you think to align with God's will, and more and more you will be able to become like Christ and know His will.

Let's bring this full-circle. What were the three main points of Romans 11:36? From Him. By Him. For Him. Our bodies came from Him, exist by Him, and are to be used for Him.

I know we have discussed a lot. But keeping this in mind, I want you to see how you can apply this practically to your life. Think about the parts of your body, how they function, and how they can be used for God's glory. And when you can, back it up with Scripture.

There's a chart on the next few pages for you to complete and I've gotten a few started for you. To help, Ephesians 4:17-32 lists several body parts and functions you can study and fill in the chart. If you want more scripture relating to a certain topic, feel free to look up body parts or functions in the concordance of your Bible to find something applicable. Or if there is a particular area you struggle with (example: lying, anger) you could look that up and find scripture to help you deal appropriately with that.

In Matthew 4, Jesus was tempted by the devil and each time He used scripture to refute the temptation to sin. This is an example to us of how to tap into the Holy Spirit's power to overcome our weaknesses. Psalm 119:11 says, "I have hidden your word in my heart, that I might not sin against you." Remember, sin has *no* power in your life if you are a believer! And as I said in the first chapter, we are to be set apart for God.

Body Part	Function	Application	Scripture
Head (mind)	Thoughts & Attitudes	Renewed by Spirit	**Philippians 4:8b (NLT)** - "Fix your thoughts on what is true, and honorable, and right, and pure, and lovely, and admirable. Think about things that are excellent and worthy of praise."
	Wisdom		**James 3:17 (ESV)** - "But the wisdom from above is first pure, then peaceable, gentle, open to reason, full of mercy and good fruits, impartial and sincere."
Eyes	Boys	No lust	**Matthew 5:27-28 (CSB)** - "You have heard that it was said, 'Do not commit adultery.' But I tell you, everyone who looks at a woman lustfully has already committed adultery with her in his heart."
	Internet/Movies/ Entertainment	No pornography	
	Books	Bible	**Psalm 119:18, 37 (CSB)** - "Open my eyes so that I may contemplate wondrous things from your instruction...turn my eyes from looking at what is worthless; give me life in your ways."

Body Part	Category	Details
Ears	Music	
	Teaching (of the Word)	**2 Timothy 4:3-4 (NLT)** - "For a time is coming when people will no longer listen to sound and wholesome teaching. They will follow their own desires and will look for teachers who will tell them whatever their itching ears want to hear. They will reject truth and chase after myths." **2 Timothy 3:16-17 (NLT)** - "All Scripture is inspired by God and is useful to teach us what is true and to make us realize what is wrong in our lives. It corrects us when we are wrong and teaches us to do what is right. God uses it to prepare and equip his people to do every good work."
Nose	Smell	• God's Creation (fresh-cut grass, flowers)
Arms/Hands	Stealing	**Ephesians 4:28 (NLT)**- "If you are a thief, quit stealing. Instead, use your hands for good hard work, and then give generously to others in need."
	Working	
	Generosity	Help others

Mouth			
	Words	Witnessing	**2 Timothy 4:5c (NLT)** – "Work at telling others the Good News, and fully carry out the ministry God has given you."
		Encouragement	
		No lying/ perverse talk	**Psalm 34:13 (NLT)** – "Then keep your tongue from speaking evil and your lips from telling lies!" **Proverbs 4:24 (NLT)** – "Avoid all perverse talk; stay away from corrupt speech."
		Thanksgiving / Praise	**Ephesians 5:20 (NLT)**– "And give thanks for everything to God the Father in the name of our Lord Jesus Christ."
		Gossip	
Heart			**Psalm 119:11 (CSB)** – "I have treasured your word in my heart so that I may not sin against you." **Proverbs 4:23 (CSB)** – "Guard your heart above all else, for it is the source of life."

Stomach	Eating/Drinking	• Make healthy choices • No gluttony

Ephesians 5:18a (CSB) - "And don't get drunk with wine, which leads to reckless living."
Proverbs 23:20-21 (CSB) - "Don't associate with those who drink too much wine or with those who gorge themselves on meat. For the drunkard and the glutton will become poor, and grogginess will clothe them in rags."

Legs/Feet	Walking / Path of Life	Exercise/Care for Body

Proverbs 4:27 (NLT) - "Don't get sidetracked; keep your feet from following evil."
1 Corinthians 9:25-26a (NLT) - "All athletes are disciplined in their training. They do it to win a prize that will fade away, but we do it for an eternal prize. So I run with purpose in every step."

Intimate Parts	God's design for purity	

1 Corinthians 6:9, 13b, 18-20 (NLT) - "Don't you realize that those who do wrong will not inherit the Kingdom of God? Don't fool yourselves. Those who indulge in sexual sin, or who worship idols, or commit adultery, or are male prostitutes or practice homosexuality ... But you can't say that our bodies were made for sexual immorality. They were made for the Lord, and the Lord cares about our bodies ... Run from sexual sin! No other sin so clearly affects the body as this one does. For sexual immorality is a sin against your own body. Don't you realize that your body is the temple of the Holy Spirit, who lives in you and was given to you by God?"

Discussion Questions

1. In Romans 12:1, why does the author use the word "bodies"?

2. What are some things Scripture tells us to do with our bodies?

3. Describe sacrifice and how it relates to the concept of purity.

4. In order to be renewed by the Holy Spirit, what must happen?

5. What are some scriptures that you can use in your own life to fight off temptations and struggles?

Chapter 5

Sexual Purity

This may be the chapter you are dreading, or thought you were reading in the last chapter, or you may be looking forward to it. We all are in different places. But because our culture has come so far away from God's design for us in purity, I am compelled to narrow our study from the last chapter on purity and specifically look at sexual purity from God's standpoint.

You may have heard some of this before. It may make you uncomfortable. It may sound outdated or "old school," but as I have previously stated, our culture changes; God does not. I am going to ask you to stick this one out to the end because as harsh as some of it sounds, there is a story of hope and redemption — but it's at the very end. Before we jump in, I want to share part of my story.

When I was growing up, I signed a sexual purity promise at the age of 13. I was more than willing to do this at that time since I had no prospects! And I agree that doing it before a relationship occurs is the best time to make such a commitment. However, there wasn't much discussion on what was acceptable and not acceptable. I knew "no sex before marriage" — but what about other things (although at that point I had no clue)?

Nearly four years later I found myself in a serious relationship. Things moved rather fast from the physical standpoint. A first kiss quickly led to making out. Time alone together "watching a movie" rapidly led to touching. We attempted to back up and discuss boundaries, but even this conversation of what was off-limits was no match for being alone together with raging teenage hormones. As time went on, we both went to college but were committed to each other. Temptation grew worse, and the opportunities to be alone together became more frequent. By this point it was almost like a habit we could not break free from. When we were around each other we would go out to dinner and a movie or bowling or whatever fun thing, but at the end of the day we found ourselves together — alone. I remember one time in particular sensing the Spirit telling me to "STOP!" And my response? I am ashamed to admit that it was, "But you are going to forgive me, right?"

My struggle was with the "gray area." I had signed a purity promise and we didn't actually have intercourse. You may be wondering "what's wrong with that?" Our culture forces us to push the limits that are in place, potentially compromise what we know is right, and think that anything related to sex is ok. However, in Matthew 5:27-28 Jesus is speaking about the seventh of the Ten Commandments and says, "You have heard the commandment that says, 'You must not commit adultery. But I say, anyone who even looks at a woman with lust has already committed adultery with her in his heart.' "

What is adultery?

Adultery is sexual unfaithfulness in marriage. And we weren't married. But in this passage, Jesus is raising the standard by saying that if you even have lustful eyes toward someone you have sinned in this way! What about that? My boyfriend and I had definitely done more than look at each other with lust!

Remember how I said at the beginning of the book that I longed to feel beautiful? The physical side of this relationship made me feel beautiful and desirable, which caused me to compromise my convictions and led further away from Christ. So I'll ask you — is there a boyfriend, lifeguard, soccer player, or rock star you look at lustfully? Those fall into this category. To God, the issue is in our hearts and the emotional versus physical is all the same to Him. Romans 3:23 (CSB), "For all have sinned and fall short of the glory of God."

You may argue "well what if we are planning to get married or are engaged?" The answer is still "not yet." I would love to tell you that for us temptation improved and we were able to stand against it, but I cannot. The day before our wedding we almost went all the way. After all, within 24 hours we would be married and sex would be ok — even expected.

First Thessalonians 4:3 says, "God's will is for you to be holy, so stay away from all sexual sin." In the last chapter we talked about being holy. This verse specifically states that the way to do that is to "stay away from all sexual sin." In the original language, the word for "sexual sin" is porneia, which means "illicit sexual intercourse, adultery, fornication, homosexuality, lesbianism, intercourse with animals, etc."[16]

We just discussed adultery, but what is fornication?

By definition, it is specifically a sexual relationship outside of marriage[17], but also encompasses prostitution and all kinds of sexual immorality[18]. Leviticus 18 presents multiple situations and specific people with whom intercourse is forbidden if you need more details.

GOD'S DESIGN FOR SEXUALITY

Our society places great emphasis on sexuality and glamorizes various sexual expressions. To avert the idea that sexuality is bad or sex is wrong, we are going to take some time to discuss God's design for sexuality and then come back to how it relates to our culture. You may be thinking, "What? God designed sexuality?" Yes he did — and He created sex. And everything He created is good. But in order for it to gain His approval, it must be used within the boundaries that He set. We find this information in the beginning of time when He first created people.

 Read Genesis 1:27-28 in your Bible.

There are two things I want to point out in these verses: 1) God created male and female; 2) He instructed them to "be fruitful and multiply," which is a command to reproduce. In the next chapter of Genesis, more detail is given about how God created man and woman. Additionally, the purpose of the woman was revealed and the first marriage occurred. Genesis 2:18 says, "Then the LORD God said, 'It is not good for man to be alone. I will make a helper who is just right for him.' " I find it humorous that immediately after God makes this statement, He then brings every single animal to Adam for him to name — every variation of every bird, every creeping thing, all the livestock, and wild animals. Then at the end of verse 20, "but still there was no helper just right for him." Don't you think after Adam finished the arduous task of naming all these creatures he was exhausted and probably in despair that he was the only one like himself? Let's continue. Genesis 2:21-25:

> "21 So the LORD God caused the man to fall into a deep sleep.
> While the man slept, the LORD God took out one of the man's
> ribs and closed up the opening.
>
> 22 Then the LORD God made a woman from the rib, and he brought
> her to the man.
>
> 23 'At last!' The man exclaimed. 'This one is bone from my bone,
> and flesh from my flesh! She will be called 'woman,' because she

was taken from man.'

24 This explains why a man leaves his father and mother and is joined to his wife, and the two are united into one.

25 Now the man and his wife were both naked, but they felt no shame."

So Adam named all these animals and God finally made him a helper. Did you catch his response? He was stunned. In awe. "WHOA! MAN!" (woman). This is the first thing I want you to see: God made his helper a woman, not another man. It just reiterates Genesis 1:27 from above.

The next thing is that his helper was made from a rib. First off, consider the location of the rib — his side. Then think about two purposes of the ribs: to support other structures and muscles, and aid in respiration. I know — how does this anatomy lesson relate to anything? Women are to partner alongside their husbands in a supportive manner and aid them — not attempt to rule over them. While we are to be submissive, we are not to be a doormat either (an entirely different lesson I am not going to delve into here).

Look back at verse 24. This is the first time the woman is addressed as "wife," so God has married the man and woman.

What does it mean for the two to be "united into one"?

The two becoming one means that God intended for marriage to occur between one man and one woman. It also means that when we get married, the sexual relationship that ensues unites us into one before God. This isn't really something that is visible or understood easily, but sex has a spiritual connection and is an intimacy that is reserved for a marriage relationship.

Lastly, verse 25 says that they were naked yet unashamed. I think this was

God's way of encouraging them to fulfill His command to "be fruitful and multiply." At this point, they did not have to work for their food; everything was provided freely. God just wanted them to have fun.

So God's design for sexuality in a nutshell: sex is to be reserved for one man and one woman in a marriage relationship, with the purpose of reproduction and unity, as well as working together, side by side to fulfill God's purpose. Now let's go back and discuss how this relates to our culture today.

CULTURE'S DEVIATION FROM GOD'S DESIGN

As we discuss sexuality in our society, it is imperative to remember God's design that we just described. It is also important to be familiar with 2 Corinthians 12:7-10. In these verses, God's most influential apostle of the New Testament, Paul, was describing a time when he prayed to God three times asking Him to remove a "thorn in the flesh." No one knows exactly what this referred to — whether a physical ailment or spiritual torment or specific temptation. Each time Paul asked, God responded with, "My grace is all you need. My power works best in weakness." Paul went on to say that he became glad about his weakness because that is when Christ's work through him was greatest. Verse 10 says, "For when I am weak, then I am strong."

We tend to think of grace in verse 9 as God's bestowing on us some divine power. I would define this as God's undeserved favor or approval. However, another meaning of grace is "that which affords pleasure, joy, delight."[19] In essence, God is saying, "I am enough. Delight in Me." This is a reciprocation. God delights in those who follow Christ. When we realize the gravity of this, our response is to delight in Him.

God chose not to remove Paul's "thorn" because it caused him to be reliant on God rather than himself. Paul had to lean into the Holy Spirit's power to overcome, and we should do the same. Remember: new life, new power. Verse 9 is a command and a promise: when we delight in Him and He in us, we have victory over our weaknesses. So we are glad about our earthly weaknesses because that is when Christ's power works in and through us, giving us more strength than we could ever have on our own! We cannot delight in God and indulge our weakness at the same time.

In our society, we are forced to confront sexuality; it is everywhere we look — commercials and advertisements, social media, news, political rallies, and even attitudes about how genders relate to each other. Our culture, however, has pushed against the boundaries set by God and the media has bombarded us with glamorized versions of various gender identities, sexual expressions, and promiscuity.

GENDER IDENTITY

While the Bible doesn't use the term "gender identity," God ordered this when He created people at the beginning of time.

 **Go back and re-read Genesis 1:27 in your Bible.**

One thing we can glean from this is that God created two genders — and contrary to our culture — only two genders.

What two genders did God create?

He did not design any form of non-binary gender and he designed gender to be biological — not a preference, and not something for us to switch depending on our feelings. Now if you are having confusing thoughts regarding this about yourself, bear with me for just a moment. I am not at all trying to isolate you; you likely feel that enough. Let's briefly talk about feelings.

Remember at the beginning I told you how my feelings led me to compromise my beliefs? I wanted what felt good in the moment, what validated my deepest longings. But I looked to a physical relationship to fulfill that rather than God. We all have a deep longing — a void, really. And we all constantly try to fill this hole in our heart with stuff. However, God is the only thing that will bring absolute fulfillment and satisfaction. God is unchanging, and who we are in His eyes is unchanging. Our feelings, on the other hand, are temporary and at times, volatile. Why would we change something so core to our identity — our gender — based on some feelings that may with time decide to be agreeable with our biological status? And even if our feelings regarding our gender do not change, if we know God and trust in His plan, He can help us stay true to His word. This struggle is no different than any other. It is no better or worse than mine: "For all have sinned and fall short of the glory of God," but "[His] grace is sufficient. [His] power works best in [our] weakness" (Romans 3:23, 2 Corinthians 12:9).

HOMOSEXUALITY

As I mentioned, sexuality in general is glamorized in our culture and more recently, homosexuality has become applauded. It is a sensitive subject, so while I am going to present Truth from God's Word, I am also going to show you His grace. Please read this section all the way through once you start it.

In Genesis 1:28, God blessed the man and woman he had created and commanded them to "be fruitful and multiply." Reproduction, however, cannot take place naturally between two people of the same gender. Therefore, homosexuality goes directly against one of God's first commands to people. The Bible speaks of homosexuality as "detestable" in the sight of God (Leviticus 18:22). It also denounces playing the part — women dressing in men's clothing and men dressing in women's clothing (Deuteronomy 22:5).

Wait, before you throw this out! I want to point out one more thing from

Scripture. First Corinthians 6:9 says, "Don't you realize that those who do wrong will not inherit the Kingdom of God? Don't fool yourselves. Those who indulge in sexual sin, or who worship idols, or commit adultery, or are male prostitutes, or practice homosexuality," but the author does not stop there! Continuing in verses 10 and 11, "or are thieves, or greedy people, or drunkards, or are abusive, or cheat people — none of these will inherit the Kingdom of God. Some of you were once like that. But you were cleansed; you were made holy; you were made right with God by calling on the name of the Lord Jesus Christ and by the Spirit of our God."

Two things I want you to see here: a level playing field and hope. Those who sin sexually are just as guilty as thieves, the greedy, drunks, abusers, cheaters, and *others who do wrong*. That includes all of us. James 2:10 says, "For the person who keeps all of the laws except one is as guilty as the person who has broken all of God's laws." In other words, sin is sin and God does not weigh our sin on a scale. It is all wrong and it all separates us from a Holy God.

Our culture encourages us to judge people with whom we disagree. As Christians, rather than judge and shame, we should love as Jesus loved us (John 13:34). After all, everyone struggles with something, but there is hope in Christ! Remember from the last chapter: new life and new power. If you struggle with homosexuality, your sin is no better or worse than mine: "For all have sinned and fall short of the glory of God," but "[His] grace is sufficient. [His] power works best in [our] weakness" (Romans 3:23, 2 Corinthians 12:9).

PROMISCUITY

 **What is promiscuity?**

Promiscuous behavior is loose, wild, or casual sexual behaviors. There is a significant amount of space dedicated to an immoral or promiscuous woman in the book of Proverbs. This book was written by the wisest man on earth — who had thousands of wives that ultimately led to his downfall! So if anyone knows anything about being seduced by a woman, it would be him. And every time he mentioned the immoral woman, he contrasted it with wisdom! Basically it is not wise to be with a promiscuous woman. He also wrote in Proverbs 5:15-17, "drink water from your own well — share your love only with your wife. Why spill the water of your springs in the streets, having sex with just anyone? You should reserve it for yourselves. Never share it with strangers." This is a picture of the intimacy that accompanies sex and how it should be enjoyed exclusively in a marriage relationship.

If you are already caught up in a promiscuous lifestyle, it can be difficult to break free from. This is why Song of Solomon 2:7 (CSB) says, "Young women of Jerusalem, I charge you … do not stir up or awaken love until the appropriate time." The word love here includes emotional love between man and woman as well as sexual desire[20]. The appropriate time as we saw earlier is marriage.

Another reason we should refrain from promiscuity is found in 1 Corinthians 6:18-20. It reminds believers to "flee sexual immorality! Every other sin a person commits is outside the body, but the person who is sexually immoral sins against his own body. Don't you know that your body is a temple of the Holy Spirit who is in you, whom you have from God? You are not your own, for you were bought at a price. So glorify God with your body." And since the Holy Spirit lives in followers of Christ, 1 Corinthians 10:13 gives us hope for defeating this temptation: "The temptations in your life are no different from what others experience. And God is faithful. He will not allow the temptation to be more than you can stand. When you are tempted, he will show you a way out so that you can endure." Remember how I sensed the Spirit telling me to stop? That was my way out. Regrettably, I did not take it. "For all have sinned and fall short of the glory of God," but "[His] grace is sufficient. [His] power works best in [our] weakness" (Romans 3:23, 2 Corinthians 12:9).

MODESTY

One area that may be easily overlooked in terms of sexual purity is modesty. I want to remind you of the modesty we discussed in chapter two where 1 Timothy 2:9 (ESV) talks about dressing "in modest and respectable clothing" and not seeking to be noticed by the way you dress. Do not solicit attention for your body or use your body to benefit you outside of a marriage relationship. These actions do not respect yourself, nor are they seeking respectful attention from others.

Romans 14:13b says, "Decide instead to live in such a way that you will not cause another believer to stumble and fall." Here is how this relates to this particular topic: do not dress or act in a way that causes someone else to lust after you. The Bible tells us that other believers are our brothers and sisters in Christ. If you consider guys you know who are believers as your "brothers," would you want your brother to look at you in lust? Furthermore, would you want to cause your brother to sin?

Do you remember at the beginning of the book I told you how I longed to be beautiful? Although I wore clothes that were modest, I began putting my self-worth in how beautiful I felt when I dressed a certain way. (Sometimes I still struggle with this — getting dressed up to go out versus wearing my raggedy paint clothes). One time in particular I had just begun this same dating relationship and I wore a top that was a little more low-cut in the front than I would normally wear. My dad said something to me about it before we left for school, but I didn't change. So he showed up to school with another shirt for me to wear that had a more modest neckline. While I was completely mortified, I see now how I was attempting to use my body to make myself desirable to others (guys — or one in particular). This longing led me to dress in order to be noticed and allowed me to be used as a stumbling block for someone who was my brother in Christ.

TO THE SEXUALLY ABUSED

You may be on a different side of this. You feel dirty and ashamed. You have been violated but not by choice. Someone stole your innocence. You may feel that you could never trust a male with intimacy because a male used you, so you have turned to find love, acceptance, and fulfillment in females. You may feel that you did something wrong or something to deserve it, although you did not. Or you may feel you cannot trust at all, so you give yourself away again and again to feel temporary love — or as punishment to yourself. In Deuteronomy 22:26, the author is listing punishments for those involved in sexual offenses. He says this of a woman who has been raped, "Do nothing to the young woman; she has committed no crime worthy of death. She is as innocent as a murder victim." Did you see that? She is innocent. God does not condemn you because someone else violated you.

At the same time, you may feel that you can't trust God because God is a "He" and so was your perpetrator. You may feel you can't trust God because if He's so loving why would He let something so bad happen? Let me clarify that God knows what happened but He didn't cause it to happen. The brokenness of this world and pain we experience are a direct result of the sin committed by the first two people (I spoke of this in chapter 3) multiplied generation after generation.

You may be thinking, "Well that was thousands of years ago. Why now? Why me?" Just as God allowed Adam and Eve to make a choice in the garden whether or not to follow his command, He allows each of us to make choices every moment of every day — whether good or bad. Your perpetrator chose to follow evil and at that moment, you happened to be present.

Know that God does not sit idly by as horrible situations occur. He grieves when people rebel and make wrong decisions (Isaiah 63:10, Psalm 78:40-42), and His Word promises that He will take vengeance on those who sin against us. Deuteronomy 22:25 tells us that God judges a sexual violator as worthy of death; however, He is the one to carry out their punishment. Romans 12:19 (CSB) says, " 'Friends, do not avenge yourselves; instead, leave room for God's wrath, because it is written, Vengeance belongs to me; I will repay,' says the Lord."

He also walks with us through difficult circumstances, promising never to abandon us (Hebrews 13:5b). In Isaiah 43:2, God is speaking to his people, "When you go through deep waters, I will be with you. When you go through rivers of difficulty, you will not drown. When you walk through the fire of oppression, you will not be burned up; the flames will not consume you."

Remember, I said bad things happen, but bad things do not come from God. James 1:17 says, "Whatever is good and perfect comes down to us from God our Father, who created all the lights in the heavens. He never changes or casts a shifting shadow." This means that at God's core being, He is fully good and perfect, and because He never changes or even hints at change, only good and perfect things can come from Him.

God's opponent Satan, however, "prowls around like a roaring lion, looking for someone to devour." (1 Peter 5:8). This is speaking of sin but — even though your situation may be the result of someone else sinning against you — Satan can and will use this to turn you against God. The following verse says, "Stand firm against him, and be strong in your faith. Remember that your Christian brothers and sisters all over the world are going through the same kind of suffering you are" (1 Peter 5:9). This tells us that we are not alone in whatever situation we face. Someone else has been there and can help you through your struggles. And in turn, you can help someone else through their pain because you have walked that path. "Give your burdens to the Lord, and He will take care of you" (Psalm 55:22).

REDEMPTION

I want to share one more story, but this one isn't mine. It is found in John 4. Jesus was traveling from Judea to Galilee and rather than go around Samaria — an area despised by Jews for their "half-breed" Samaritan race — He went through Samaria. Around noon, He found himself at a well and sat to rest. About this time a Samaritan woman came to the well to draw water. She had previously had five husbands and was living with a man to whom she was not married. A conversation ensued between Jesus and this woman.

In this conversation, Jesus (1) offered his gift of living water and eternal life to the woman; (2) acknowledged the lifestyle she lived before she even admitted to it; (3) pointed out her sin; (4) showed her that salvation was for all people, not only Jews; and (5) revealed himself as Messiah — Savior from sins. Initially, the woman had a difficult time seeing past the literal and recognizing Who was in front of her and what He was offering. However at the end of the day, she ran back to her village and proclaimed Jesus and many more believed in Him because of her testimony.

So what does this have to do with you? If you are currently living a lifestyle that does not align with God's design — or someone has stolen that from you, Jesus knows where you are and where you have been. Remember from chapter 1: He sees you. He offers His saving Grace to us all. As I mentioned in chapter 3, you can be made into Jesus' spotless bride. You are still worth it! Don't consider yourself as defiled or beyond God's reach and think "what difference does it make now?" You can be redeemed — and your story can be used to help someone else in their struggles. Second Corinthians 1:3-4 says, "God is our merciful Father and the source of all comfort. He comforts us in all our troubles so that we can comfort others." The question is where is your heart? Seek to please the Lord and use your body to honor Him. Don't do what I did and take advantage of God's grace and continue to stumble over the past.

BOUNDARIES

I mentioned at the beginning that I had signed a purity promise. While signing an agreement is a good idea, other preventive measures need to be in place before temptation becomes a problem. Accountability is one very important measure. I am fully convinced that if my (now) husband and I had accountability partners early-on in our relationship, things would not have continued down the path of shame and regret. Find someone you trust who will not judge you, will keep your information confidential, and will encourage you spiritually — not just say "its ok." This may need to be an adult depending on your friend circle. The Bible tells us in James 5:16 to "confess your sins to each other and pray for each other so that you may be healed."

I'm going to offer a couple of suggestions for preventive measures based on my situation, but boundaries may be different depending on your specific struggles. In our relationship (and any potentially sexual relationship) sexual temptation was strongest when we were alone together. So our first boundary should have been to not be alone and have a plan for our time together.

Another preventive measure is to discuss physical boundaries early-on in the relationship — like first date. I know, you don't want to scare him off! Excuse my bluntness, but — anyone who walks away from a relationship just because you won't give him what's in your pants — well, now you know that is all he wanted anyway. He does not respect you and has lost sight of God! In our relationship, we both knew what we were doing was wrong. We discussed the guilt we felt after indulging. We both promised not to do it again. However, we did not tap into the Holy Spirit's power to help us overcome.

When setting physical boundaries, remember Jesus's stance on lust and adultery, rather than our culture's idea that "everything is ok." In the heat of the moment, things can escalate very quickly. I would encourage you to back the boundary line up so that if you cross it, you aren't on the fast track to a path of destruction, shame, and regret. Proverbs 16:17 says, "The path of the virtuous leads away from evil; whoever follows that path is safe."

✿ What does the word "virtuous" mean?

Another word for virtuous is "righteous," which means "acting in accord with divine or moral law."[21] That is, how God designed it. Proverbs 18:22 says, "A man who finds a wife finds a treasure, and he receives favor from the Lord." The way you act now, matters for later. Train yourself now to be a wife, a treasure, virtuous.

✿ At this point I encourage you to do another self-evaluation. Are there any areas where you struggle, or are acting, or are pushing the boundary of acting outside of God's design?

✿ What are boundaries you can put in place to prevent this?

✿ Do you need forgiveness, restoration, or healing?

Run to God who loves you dearly! He is waiting with open arms. All you have to do is tell Him that you need Him to make you whole; you need His power to help you overcome in your time of weakness. Then seek Him. Read His word and foster that relationship with Him. Surround yourself with those who can encourage you on your faith journey.

If you are caught up in any of these areas we discussed, trust me it is very difficult to break loose of it. But as I mentioned in the last chapter, if you are a believer, you have new life and new power to overcome. In Matthew 5:29-30 Jesus is speaking specifically of wayward sexual relationship and says, "So if your eye — even your good eye — causes you to lust, gouge it out and throw it away. It is better for you to lose one part of your body than for your whole body to be thrown into hell. And if your hand — even your stronger hand — causes you to sin, cut it off and throw it away. It is better for you to lose one part of your body than for your whole body to be thrown into hell." Is this literal or figurative? Maybe it depends. The point is that we should be willing to cut ourselves off from anything that leads us to sin. If it's an internet connection — cut it off. If it's a certain group of friends — cut them off. If it's a particular relationship or time by yourself with someone — cut it off. Remember: From Him. By Him. For Him. All glory to Him!

Discussion Questions

1. What two genders did God create?

2. What does it mean for the two to become one flesh?

3. In your own words what is the meaning of the word virtuous?

4. What are the metaphors used that describe the promiscuous woman and what she leads to?

5. List the things the author says you will lose if you submit to the promiscuous woman.

6. Are there any areas where you struggle or am acting or pushing the boundary of acting outside of God's design?

7. What are some boundaries you can put in place to prevent yourself from going down a path of destruction?

Epilogue

In closing, I hope these lessons taught you something you didn't know about God. About yourself. About His value of you. His plans for you. I hope you understand that He is good and He loves you so much!

He wants you to live for Him, but first you must know Him. When you live your life for God and find joy in Him, that joy will show on your face and in your actions and you will radiate beauty to others. Do not seek attention from your peers. Seek attention from your Heavenly Father who loves you unconditionally and created you with such care. If you don't believe in the God who created you, then all of this we have discussed is worthless to you. Remember: From Him. By Him. For Him! All glory to Him!

References

1. "H7069 - qanah - Strong's Hebrew Lexicon (NASB)." Blue Letter Bible. Accessed 17 September, 2016. https://www.blueletterbible.org//lang/lexicon/lexicon.cfm?Strongs=H7069&t=NASB

2. "H3372 - yare' - Strong's Hebrew Lexicon (NASB)." Blue Letter Bible. Accessed 17 September, 2016. https://www.blueletterbible.org//lang/lexicon/lexicon.cfm?Strongs=H3372&t=NASB

3. "H6395 - palah - Strong's Hebrew Lexicon (NASB)." Blue Letter Bible. Accessed 17 September, 2016. https://www.blueletterbible.org//lang/lexicon/lexicon.cfm?Strongs=H6395&t=NASB

4. "H4639 - ma`aseh - Strong's Hebrew Lexicon (NASB)." Blue Letter Bible. Accessed 17 September, 2016. https://www.blueletterbible.org//lang/lexicon/lexicon.cfm?Strongs=H4639&t=NASB

5. "H3966 - m@`od - Strong's Hebrew Lexicon (NASB)." Blue Letter Bible. Accessed 17 September, 2016. https://www.blueletterbible.org//lang/lexicon/lexicon.cfm?Strongs=H3966&t=NASB

6. "H5643 - cether - Strong's Hebrew Lexicon (NASB)." Blue Letter Bible. Accessed 17 September, 2016. https://www.blueletterbible.org//lang/lexicon/lexicon.cfm?Strongs=H5643&t=NASB

7. "H7551 - raqam - Strong's Hebrew Lexicon (NASB)." Blue Letter Bible. Accessed 17 September, 2016. https://www.blueletterbible.org//lang/lexicon/lexicon.cfm?Strongs=H7551&t=NASB

8. "H3605 - kol - Strong's Hebrew Lexicon (NASB)." Blue Letter Bible. Accessed 17 September, 2016. https://www.blueletterbible.org//lang/lexicon/lexicon.cfm?Strongs=H3605&t=NASB

9. "H3789 - kathab - Strong's Hebrew Lexicon (NASB)." Blue Letter Bible.

Accessed 17 September, 2016. https://www.blueletterbible.org//lang/lexicon/lexicon.cfm?Strongs=H3789&t=NASB

10. "H3335 - yatsar - Strong's Hebrew Lexicon (NASB)." Blue Letter Bible. Accessed 17 September, 2016. https://www.blueletterbible.org//lang/lexicon/lexicon.cfm?Strongs=H3335&t=NASB

11. "H3365 - yaqar - Strong's Hebrew Lexicon (NASB)." Blue Letter Bible. Accessed 17 September, 2016. https://www.blueletterbible.org//lang/lexicon/lexicon.cfm?Strongs=H3365&t=NASB

12. "H7454 - rea` - Strong's Hebrew Lexicon (NASB)." Blue Letter Bible. Accessed 17 September, 2016. https://www.blueletterbible.org//lang/lexicon/lexicon.cfm?Strongs=H7454&t=NASB

13. McKinley, David H. "Grow Up: Sustaining Grace." Sermon, Warren Baptist Church, Augusta, February 12, 2017.

14. "Purple." *ATS Bible Dictionary*. Accessed 17 September, 2016. https://biblehub.com/topical/p/purple.htm#amt

15. Life Application Study Bible. NLT, 2nd ed. Carol Stream, IL: Tyndale House Publishers, 2007. 1058.

16. "G4202 - porneia - Strong's Greek Lexicon (NASB)." Blue Letter Bible. Accessed 5 August, 2018. https://www.blueletterbible.org//lang/lexicon/lexicon.cfm?Strongs=G4202&t=NASB

17. "fornication." *Merriam-Webster.com*. 2018. https://www.merriam-webster.com/dictionary/fornication

18. Brand, Chad, Eric Alan Mitchell, Steve Bond, E. Ray Clendenen, Trent C. Butler, and Bill Latta, eds. *Holman Illustrated Bible Dictionary*. Revised & Expanded ed. Nashville, TN: B&H Publishing, 2015. 590-91.

19. "G5485 - charis - Strong's Greek Lexicon (NASB)." Blue Letter Bible. Accessed 5 August, 2018. https://www.blueletterbible.org//lang/lexicon/lexicon.cfm?Strongs=G5485&t=NASB

20. "H160 - 'ahabah - Strong's Hebrew Lexicon (NASB)." Blue Letter Bible.

Accessed 5 August, 2018. https://www.blueletterbible.org//lang/lexicon/lexicon.cfm?Strongs=H160&t=NASB

21. "righteous." *Merriam-Webster.com*. 2018. https://www.merriam-webster.com/dictionary/righteous

Made in the USA
Columbia, SC
31 May 2022

61142082R00041